SAINSBURY'S RECIPE LIBRARY

SEASONAL
SOUPS &
STARTERS

D1369176

SAINSBURY'S RECIPE LIBRARY

SEASONAL
SOUPS &
STARTERS

MARY CADOGAN

CONTENTS

Published exclusively for J Sainsbury plc
Stamford House Stamford Street
London SE1 9LL
by Martin Books
Simon & Schuster Consumer Group
Grafton House, 64 Maids Causeway
Cambridge CB5 8DD

ISBN 0 85941 834 0
First published 1987
First paperback edition 1992
© Woodhead-Faulkner (Publishers) Ltd 1987
Printed and bound by Butler & Tanner, Frome, Somerset

INTRODUCTION

This book isn't simply a collection of first course recipes. I love starters so much, with their tantalizing promise of what is to come, that I often serve two, or even three, and forget a main course altogether. I may start with a soup or a creamy dip, go on to a vegetable or salad, then follow with a more substantial starter. I find starters offer so much scope for pretty presentation.

Alternatively you could make several starters to serve together, buffet-style. For dishes to serve with drinks, try Herbed Yogurt Cheese with Radishes and Garlic Toast, Fried Potato Skins or Pakoras with Fresh Mint Chutney.

I have grouped the recipes into seasons to help you enjoy fresh produce when it is at its best, most flavoursome and often cheapest. Having a wealth of produce from around the world to choose from has blurred the seasons somewhat, giving us treats such as strawberries at Christmas. But as each season arrives, it still brings special pleasures. There's nothing quite like the taste of the first home-grown tomatoes and bunches of radishes to herald summer.

As the days draw in, the autumn tones of golds and reds are reflected in pumpkins and squashes of all shapes and sizes, sweet red-skinned onions and an array of nuts in their shells. Try Pumpkin Soup to keep out the first chill.

Root vegetables still belong firmly to winter – parsnips, celeriac and swedes conjure up images of heart-warming soups and creamy purées to help keep out the cold. My favourites are Spiced Parsnip and Carrot and Celeriac.

Spring brings with it a feeling of renewal, and the root crops make way for the more delicate flavours of young spinach leaves, tiny new carrots, tender lettuces and the first fresh herbs. Carrot and Herb Salad is simply sweet new carrots flavoured with a posy of fresh herbs.

Tuck into these recipes, whatever the season. Try them on family, friends or just for yourself. But please, above all, eat and enjoy them.

NOTES

Ingredients are given in both metric and imperial measures. Use either set of quantities but not a mixture of both in any one recipe.

All spoon measurements are level:
1 tablespoon = one 15 ml spoon
1 teaspoon = one 5 ml spoon.

Ovens should be preheated to the temperature specified.

Freshly ground black pepper is intended where pepper is listed.

Fresh herbs are used unless otherwise stated. If unobtainable dried herbs can be substituted in cooked dishes but halve the quantities.

Eggs are standard size 3 unless otherwise stated.

Basic stocks and accompaniments are marked with an asterisk and given in the reference section (pages 78–9).

SPRING VEGETABLES WITH WARM MINT DRESSING

The vegetables I have suggested here can be varied according to the season, but they must always be perfectly fresh as their individual flavours are most important in this simple dish.

125 g (4 oz) broccoli
125 g (4 oz) French beans
175 g (6 oz) baby carrots
50 g (2 oz) mangetouts
1–2 small cooked
   beetroots, sliced thinly
few radicchio leaves
250 g (8 oz) tiny new
   potatoes, boiled in their
   skins

FOR THE DRESSING:
50 g (2 oz) unsalted butter
4 spring onions, chopped
1 tablespoon chopped mint
150 ml (1/4 pint) vegetable
   stock*
6 tablespoons dry white
   wine
142 ml (5 fl oz) carton
   whipping cream
salt and pepper to taste

Serves 4
Preparation time:
30 minutes
Cooking time:
6 minutes
Freezing:
Not recommended

1. Break the broccoli into small florets. Peel and thinly slice the stalks. Cook the broccoli, beans and carrots together in boiling salted water for 5 minutes. Add the mangetouts and cook for 1 minute. Drain and cool quickly under running cold water.
2. Arrange all the vegetables in small groups on 4 individual plates.
3. Melt 15 g (½ oz) of the butter in a saucepan, add the spring onions and mint and cook for about 1 minute.
4. Add the stock, wine and cream and bring to the boil, stirring constantly. Simmer until reduced by one third, then stir in the remaining butter, a teaspoon at a time, until the sauce is thickened and glossy. Season with pepper, and salt if necessary. Keep warm.
5. Just before serving, pour the warm sauce over the vegetables.

COURGETTE AND HAM STIR-FRY

25 g (1 oz) butter
1 teaspoon oil
1 clove garlic, chopped finely
500 g (1 lb) courgettes, cut into thin sticks

125 g (4 oz) ham, cut into strips
3 tablespoons single cream
salt and pepper to taste

Serves 4
Preparation time:
10 minutes
Cooking time:
5 minutes
Freezing:
Not recommended

1. Melt the butter and oil in a frying pan, add the garlic and fry for a few seconds. Add the courgettes and cook, stirring, for about 2 minutes, until just softened. Stir in the ham and heat through.
2. Lower the heat and stir in the cream, and salt and pepper. Serve piping hot, with soft warm bread for mopping up the juices.

COURGETTE SOUFFLÉS

These light airy soufflés make a surprisingly filling starter. When they are available, use a mixture of yellow and green courgettes.

50 g (2 oz) butter
350 g (12 oz) small courgettes, grated
25 g (1 oz) plain flour
150 ml (¼ pint) milk
1 teaspoon chopped tarragon

50 g (2 oz) Gruyère cheese, grated
3 eggs, separated
salt and pepper to taste
tarragon sprigs to garnish

Serves 4
Preparation time:
30 minutes
Cooking time:
25 minutes
Freezing:
Not recommended

1. Melt half of the butter in a small pan, add the courgettes and fry gently until softened. Remove from the heat.
2. Melt the remaining butter in a saucepan, add the flour and cook for 1 minute. Gradually stir in the milk, until thickened and smooth.
3. Remove from the heat and stir in the courgettes, tarragon, cheese, egg yolks, and salt and pepper. Whisk the egg whites until stiff, then fold carefully into the courgette mixture.
4. Divide between 4 greased 300 ml (½ pint) ovenproof dishes and bake in a preheated oven, 190°C/375°F/Gas Mark 5, for 25 minutes, until well risen and browned. Serve immediately, garnished with tarragon sprigs.

CARROT AND HERB SALAD

The beauty of this recipe is its simplicity, but to succeed it must be made with only the youngest and sweetest carrots and the freshest of herbs.

500 g (1 lb) carrots, grated
1 teaspoon lemon juice
1 tablespoon chopped
   mixed herbs, e.g. chervil,
   tarragon, mint, parsley

2 tablespoons snipped
   chives
1 teaspoon Dijon mustard
3 tablespoons olive oil
salt and pepper to taste

Serves 4
Preparation time:
15 minutes
Freezing:
Not recommended

1. Pile the carrots onto 4 individual plates. Place the lemon juice, herbs, mustard, and salt and pepper in a bowl and mix well. Stir in the olive oil.
2. Just before serving, spoon the dressing over the carrots.

SMOKED MACKEREL AND ORANGE SALAD

The tiny alfalfa sprouts go particularly well with smoked mackerel and orange, but if you cannot obtain them use beansprouts instead.

2 oranges
2 heads chicory, shredded
1 carton alfalfa sprouts
1 Little Gem lettuce
250 g (8 oz) smoked
   mackerel, skinned and
   flaked

2 teaspoons creamed
   horseradish
3 tablespoons natural set
   yogurt
salt and pepper to taste
orange slices to garnish

Serves 4
Preparation time:
15 minutes
Freezing:
Not recommended

1. Peel the oranges, discarding all pith. Cut into segments over a small bowl to catch the juice; set the juice aside. Cut each orange segment in half and place in a bowl with the chicory and alfalfa sprouts. Mix well.
2. Arrange the lettuce on 4 individual plates and spoon the chicory mixture in the centre. Top with the smoked mackerel.
3. Place 1 tablespoon of the reserved orange juice in a bowl, add the horseradish, yogurt, and salt and pepper and whisk together with a fork.
4. Drizzle a little dressing over each salad and garnish with orange slices to serve.

WILTED SPINACH AND EGG SALAD

2 eggs
350 g (12 oz) young
  spinach leaves, shredded
8 radishes, sliced
1 avocado, peeled and
  chopped
4 tablespoons oil

2 shallots, chopped
4 rashers streaky bacon,
  derinded and chopped
1 teaspoon Dijon mustard
1 tablespoon white wine
  vinegar
pepper to taste

1. Boil the eggs for 5 minutes, then shell and cool quickly. Cut each one in half.
2. Divide the spinach between 4 individual plates and top with the radishes, avocado and egg.
3. Heat 1 tablespoon of the oil in a small saucepan, add the shallots and bacon and fry for about 5 minutes, until the bacon is crisp. Lower the heat and stir in the mustard, vinegar, pepper and remaining oil. Pour evenly over each salad. Serve immediately.

Serves 4
Preparation time:
30 minutes
Freezing:
Not recommended

SMOKED SALMON AND ASPARAGUS TERRINE

*250 g (8 oz) smoked
    salmon*
*250 g (8 oz) asparagus,
    cooked lightly*
*227 g (8 oz) carton curd
    cheese*
*1 teaspoon chopped
    tarragon*

*1 tablespoon snipped
    chives*
25 g (1 oz) butter, melted
1 tablespoon lemon juice
salt and pepper to taste
lettuce leaves to garnish

Serves 4–6
Preparation time:
35 minutes, plus
chilling
Freezing:
Recommended

1. Line a 500 g (1 lb) loaf tin with smoked salmon, trimming the edges to neaten, but leaving enough to fold over the finished terrine. Set aside 3 asparagus spears.
2. Chop the remaining smoked salmon and asparagus, place in a food processor or blender and work together until fairly smooth. Add the remaining ingredients and work together until smooth.
3. Spread half of the mixture in the prepared tin and place the reserved asparagus on top, trimming the spears to the length of the tin if necessary. Cover with the remaining mixture and smooth the top.
4. Fold over the smoked salmon and cover with foil. Chill for several hours, or overnight if possible, until firm. Turn out and cut into slices, using a sharp knife. Serve garnished with lettuce leaves.

SORREL ROULADE WITH PRAWNS

Sorrel has a slightly astringent taste that goes well with all fish dishes. It is easy to grow, but if you don't have it, spinach is a good substitute. The roulade and accompanying sauce are delicious served hot or cold.

500 g (1 lb) sorrel
pinch of grated nutmeg
*50 g (2 oz) Gruyère cheese,
    grated*
4 eggs, separated
*500 g (1 lb) ripe tomatoes,
    skinned*
pinch of sugar

*2 tablespoons tomato
    purée with basil*
1 tablespoon lemon juice
*175 g (6 oz) peeled prawns
    (thawed if frozen)*
1 teaspoon chopped dill
salt and pepper to taste
dill sprigs to garnish

1. Grease and line a 33 × 23 cm (13 × 9 inch) Swiss roll tin.

2. Cook the sorrel in a covered pan with just the water clinging to the leaves after washing for about 5 minutes, until just wilted. Drain well, pressing out as much water as possible. Chop finely, then mix with the nutmeg, cheese, egg yolks, and salt and pepper.

3. Whisk the egg whites until stiff, fold into the sorrel mixture, then transfer to the prepared tin; shake to level the mixture. Cook in a preheated oven, 190°C/375°F/Gas Mark 5, for about 15 minutes, until firm.

4. Meanwhile, place the tomatoes, sugar, tomato purée, lemon juice, and salt and pepper in a pan. Simmer, uncovered, for about 10 minutes, until pulpy. Press through a sieve, then mix half with the prawns and dill. Keep both sauces warm.

5. Invert the roulade onto a sheet of greaseproof paper. Carefully remove the lining paper, then spread the prawn mixture over the roulade. Roll up carefully from a short end, using the paper to help you.

6. Cut into slices and arrange on individual plates. Spoon over a little tomato sauce and garnish with dill.

Serves 4–6
Preparation time:
45 minutes
Cooking time:
About 15 minutes
Freezing:
Not recommended

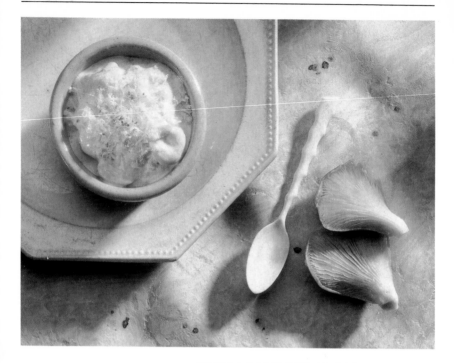

CREAMY PRAWN POTS

Oyster mushrooms are very tender and need only the
briefest cooking time.

175 g (6 oz) peeled prawns
  (thawed if frozen)
1/2 teaspoon paprika
2 teaspoons cornflour
25 g (1 oz) butter
250 g (8 oz) oyster
  mushrooms, halved if
  large

142 ml (5 fl oz) carton
  soured cream
1 tablespoon breadcrumbs
1 tablespoon grated
  Parmesan cheese
salt and pepper to taste

Serves 4
Preparation time:
10 minutes
Cooking time:
About 5 minutes
Freezing:
Not recommended

1. Mix together the prawns, paprika and cornflour. Melt
the butter in a saucepan, add the prawns and fry, stirring,
until heated through.
2. Add the mushrooms and stir-fry for 1 minute. Add the
soured cream, and salt and pepper and heat through
gently, stirring constantly.
3. Divide the mixture between 4 ramekin dishes. Mix
together the breadcrumbs and cheese and sprinkle over
the top. Place under a preheated hot grill for about
2 minutes, until the top is crisp and golden. Serve hot.

SOLE ROLL-UPS WITH ALMOND SAUCE

The almond sauce is Middle Eastern in origin. Its delicate flavour is perfect with any baked or grilled fish.

4 sole fillets, skinned
3 tablespoons lemon juice
50 g (2 oz) ground
*   almonds*
300 ml (½ pint) chicken
*   stock**
1 clove garlic, crushed

½ teaspoon turmeric
1 tablespoon chopped
*   parsley*
salt and pepper to taste
shredded lemon rind to
*   garnish*

1. Season the sole fillets with salt, pepper and 1 table-spoon of the lemon juice. Roll up and place in a greased dish. Cover with foil and cook in a preheated oven, 180°C/350°F/Gas Mark 4, for 15–18 minutes, until tender.
2. Meanwhile, prepare the sauce. Place the remaining lemon juice in a saucepan with the almonds, stock, garlic and turmeric. Bring to the boil, then simmer for 10 minutes, until thickened. Season with salt and pepper and stir in the parsley.
3. Divide the sauce between 4 individual warmed plates. Drain the fish on kitchen paper and place in the centre. Garnish with lemon rind to serve.

Serves 4
Preparation time:
25 minutes
Cooking time:
15–18 minutes
Freezing:
Not recommended

POTTED HAM WITH PARSLEY

Ideally, this dish should be made the day before it is to be served to allow the flavours to develop. It will keep well in the refrigerator for up to 5 days.

500 g (1 lb) piece mild
cure bacon or gammon
150 ml (¼ pint) dry white
wine
2 cloves
few celery leaves
1 small onion, quartered

6 black peppercorns
1 bay leaf
3 parsley sprigs
1 tablespoon lemon juice
2 teaspoons gelatine
4 tablespoons chopped
parsley

Serves 4–6
Preparation time:
25 minutes, plus
chilling
Cooking time:
1½ hours
Freezing:
Not recommended

1. Cut the bacon into 2.5 cm (1 inch) cubes. Place in a saucepan with the wine, cloves, celery leaves, onion, peppercorns, bay leaf and parsley sprigs. Cover with water and bring to the boil.
2. Remove any scum that rises to the surface with a slotted spoon, then cover and simmer for 1½ hours, until the bacon is very tender. Strain, reserving the stock.
3. Flake the bacon finely with a knife and fork and pack into a serving bowl.
4. Measure 300 ml (½ pint) of the stock, place in a small pan with the lemon juice and bring to the boil. Remove from the heat and sprinkle over the gelatine, stirring until dissolved. Add half of the chopped parsley, then pour over the bacon. Cool, then chill until set.
5. Sprinkle with the remaining parsley and serve with Suffolk Rusks* and a few salad leaves.

CHICKEN SATÉ

500 g (1 lb) boneless
chicken breasts, skinned
and cut into thin strips
1 teaspoon turmeric
1 tablespoon lemon juice
salt and pepper to taste
cucumber and onion slices
to serve
FOR THE SAUCE:
75 g (3 oz) creamed
coconut
300 ml (½ pint) boiling
water

2 cloves garlic
1 onion, chopped
2 red chillies, halved,
seeded and chopped
roughly
2 tablespoons oil
3 tablespoons lemon juice
1 tablespoon light brown
soft sugar
125 g (4 oz) peanut
kernels, toasted and
ground

1. Place the chicken, turmeric, lemon juice, and salt and pepper in a bowl and mix well. Leave to marinate while preparing the sauce.

2. Grate the coconut into a bowl, add the water and stir until smooth.

3. Place the garlic, onion, chillies and 1 tablespoon of the coconut water in a food processor or blender and work together until smooth.

4. Heat the oil in a frying pan, add the chilli mixture and fry for 2–3 minutes, stirring constantly. Stir in the lemon juice, sugar, remaining coconut water, and salt to taste. Stir well, add the ground peanuts and simmer for 2–3 minutes, until thickened. Remove from the heat, leave to cool, then place in a serving bowl or 4 individual dishes.

5. Thread the chicken onto 16–20 bamboo skewers and cook under a preheated medium grill for 6–8 minutes, turning once, until just cooked. Serve with the peanut sauce and cucumber and onion slices.

Serves 4
Preparation time:
35 minutes
Cooking time:
6–8 minutes
Freezing:
Not recommended

CHILLED ALMOND AND GRAPE SOUP

This soup from southern Spain has a delicate flavour.

75 g (3 oz) blanched almonds
4 cloves garlic
1 tablespoon olive oil
1 tablespoon white wine vinegar
125 g (4 oz) day-old white bread, crusts removed

900 ml (1½ pints) water or chicken stock*
1 tablespoon chopped parsley
350 g (12 oz) white grapes, halved and seeded
salt and pepper to taste
ice cubes to serve

Serves 4
Preparation time:
30 minutes
Freezing:
Not recommended

1. Place the almonds, garlic, oil and vinegar in a food processor or blender and work together until smooth. Add the bread and water or stock, a little at a time, and work until smooth. Season with salt and pepper.
2. Pour into a large serving bowl and stir in the parsley and grapes. Serve in individual bowls, with ice cubes.

SPRING VEGETABLE SOUP WITH PESTO

Mixed vegetable soups are great for using up any leftover vegetables—this list is flexible. Pesto is an Italian basil sauce, available ready-made in jars.

1 tablespoon olive oil
2 rashers streaky bacon, derinded and chopped
2 leeks, chopped
2 carrots, chopped
2 celery sticks, chopped
1 green pepper, cored, seeded and chopped

50 g (2 oz) cauliflower, broken into florets
1 potato, chopped
397 g (14 oz) can chopped tomatoes
900 ml (1½ pints) vegetable stock*
2 tablespoons pesto
salt and pepper to taste

Serves 4
Preparation time:
25 minutes
Cooking time:
20 minutes
Freezing:
Recommended

1. Heat the oil in a large saucepan, add the bacon and fry for about 5 minutes, until crisp. Add the fresh vegetables and turn in the oil until evenly coated.
2. Stir in the tomatoes and stock. Bring to the boil, cover and simmer for 20 minutes, until the vegetables are tender.
3. Purée one third of the soup in a food processor or blender, return to the pan and reheat gently. Season with salt and pepper and stir in the pesto. Serve piping hot with Cheese Sticks*.

BROCCOLI SOUP WITH YOGURT

This soup must be made to order as it rapidly loses its fresh
taste and colour on standing.

500 g (1 lb) broccoli
25 g (1 oz) butter
1 onion, chopped
1 potato, chopped
*1 teaspoon grated fresh
   root ginger*
juice of 1 lime

*900 ml (1½ pints) chicken
   stock**
*150 g (5.3 oz) carton
   natural yogurt*
1 tablespoon oil
1 teaspoon sesame seeds
salt and pepper to taste

Serves 4
Preparation time:
20 minutes
Cooking time:
20–25 minutes
Freezing:
Not recommended

1. Cut the broccoli into florets. Slice the stalks thinly. Set
aside 25 g (1 oz) small florets for garnish.
2. Melt the butter in a large saucepan, add the onion and
fry until softened. Add the broccoli, potato and ginger and
stir well.
3. Add the lime juice, stock, and salt and pepper. Bring to
the boil, then cover and simmer for 20–25 minutes, until
the broccoli is tender.
4. Purée in a food processor or blender, return to the pan
and reheat gently. Check the seasoning. Carefully stir in
the yogurt and heat through, making sure the soup does
not boil.
5. Meanwhile, heat the oil in a small pan, add the reserved
broccoli and stir-fry for 2 minutes. Sprinkle with the
sesame seeds and stir well.
6. Transfer the soup to 4 individual warmed bowls and
top with the broccoli florets. Serve immediately.

MALAYSIAN KING PRAWN SOUP

The hot, spicy and sour flavours in this soup will certainly
tingle your taste buds! Serve it as part of a spicy meal.

*500 g (1 lb) uncooked
   king prawns*
1 tablespoon oil
*1.2 litres (2 pints) boiling
   water*
2 cloves garlic, crushed
*2 stalks lemon grass
   (optional)*
2 tablespoons chilli sauce

1 tablespoon lime juice
2 tablespoons lemon juice
*2 tablespoons finely
   chopped spring onion*
*1 red chilli, seeded and
   chopped finely*
*1 tablespoon chopped
   coriander leaves*
salt to taste

1. Shell the prawns and reserve the heads. Cut the prawns down the back to remove the digestive tract. Rinse the heads well and dry on kitchen paper.

2. Heat the oil in a saucepan, add the prawn heads and fry until they turn pink. Add the boiling water, garlic, lemon grass if using, chilli sauce and lime juice. Bring to the boil, then cover and simmer for 25 minutes. Strain the stock and return to the pan with the lemon juice and salt.

3. Just before serving, add the prawns and simmer until pink. Stir in half the spring onion, chilli and coriander leaves and hand the remainder in a separate bowl to serve.

Serves 4
Preparation time:
20 minutes
Cooking time:
25 minutes
Freezing:
Recommended

WATERCRESS AND CHICKEN SOUP

The success of this soup depends greatly on the quality of the stock, so it is not one where you can cheat with cubes. Japanese soy sauce is also called shoyu; it has a more subtle flavour than Chinese soy sauce.

250 g (8 oz) skinned
boneless chicken breast
2 tablespoons dry sherry or
rice wine
1.2 litres (2 pints) chicken
stock*

1 tablespoon Japanese soy
sauce
1 bunch watercress,
chopped roughly
salt to taste

Serves 4
Preparation time:
15 minutes
Cooking time:
8 minutes
Freezing:
Not recommended

1. Slice the chicken into wafer-thin slivers across the grain. Place in a bowl and sprinkle with the sherry or rice wine and a little salt.
2. Bring the stock and soy sauce to the boil. Add the chicken, cover and simmer for 5 minutes. Add the watercress and simmer for 1 minute. Serve immediately.

MINTED PEA SOUP

This soup is a good way of using peas when they are plentiful and cheap. If you use home-grown peas, don't discard the pods—wash them and simmer in the stock for 30 minutes, then strain and use as directed below—they improve the flavour of the soup.

50 g (2 oz) butter
2 shallots, chopped
2 celery sticks, chopped
1 tablespoon chopped mint
500 g (1 lb) fresh peas
900 ml (1 ½ pints) chicken
or vegetable stock*

⅓ cucumber, peeled and
diced
½ cos lettuce, shredded
salt and pepper to taste
mint sprigs to garnish

Serves 4
Preparation time:
35 minutes
Cooking time:
25 minutes
Freezing:
Not recommended

1. Melt the butter in a large saucepan, add the shallots and celery and fry gently until softened. Stir in the mint and peas and cook for 1 minute.
2. Add the stock, bring to the boil, then cover and simmer for 15 minutes. Add the cucumber, lettuce, and salt and pepper and simmer for 10 minutes.
3. Purée half of the soup in a food processor or blender, then return to the pan. Serve piping hot, garnished with mint sprigs.

MINTED AVOCADO DIP

Avocado flesh discolours quickly, but if you place the stone in the prepared dip and cover with clingfilm it will stay green for a few hours.

2 ripe avocados
2 tablespoons lemon juice
2 tablespoons natural
yogurt
1 clove garlic, crushed

1 tablespoon chopped mint
salt and pepper to taste
TO SERVE:
4–6 pitta breads
mint sprigs

Serves 4
Preparation time:
15 minutes
Freezing:
Not recommended

1. Halve and stone the avocados. Spoon the flesh into a bowl and mash with a fork until soft and smooth.
2. Stir in the remaining ingredients and mix well. Turn into a serving dish or onto 4 individual plates.
3. Grill the pitta breads on both sides and cut into halves or fingers. Garnish the avocado dip with mint sprigs and serve with the warm pitta bread.

LATE SUMMER SALAD

Give yourself plenty of time to prepare and arrange the vegetables for this colourful salad. Serve with lots of freshly ground black pepper.

¼ small red cabbage,
shredded finely
1 sweetcorn cob, cooked
and sliced into rings
175 g (6 oz) each raw
beetroot and courgettes,
cut into matchstick
pieces
125 g (4 oz) cup
mushrooms, sliced thinly

125 g (4 oz) shelled cob
nuts
2 tablespoons tarragon
vinegar
4 tablespoons hazelnut oil
1 tablespoon Greek
strained yogurt
1 teaspoon Dijon mustard
salt and pepper to taste

Serves 4
Preparation time:
30 minutes
Freezing:
Not recommended

1. Arrange the vegetables in neat piles on 4 individual plates. Sprinkle the nuts over the top.
2. Whisk the remaining ingredients together with a fork until thick. Drizzle over the salads just before serving.

MARINATED ARTICHOKES WITH SALAMI

Sprinkle the artichokes with lemon juice as you prepare them to prevent discoloration. When they are not in season—or are too expensive—use a 400 g (14 oz) can artichoke hearts, well drained and rinsed.

4–6 globe artichokes
4 tablespoons lemon juice
2 tablespoons olive oil
1 tablespoon chopped
  parsley

2 teaspoons chopped
  coriander leaves
125 g (4 oz) Italian
  salami, sliced thinly
salt and pepper to taste
lemon slices to garnish

Serves 4
Preparation time:
30 minutes, plus chilling
Cooking time:
20–25 minutes
Freezing:
Not recommended

1. Remove the artichoke stalks and peel off the tough outer leaves, until you reach the tender yellow leaves. Cut off and discard the top two thirds of the leaves, using a stainless steel knife. Peel the base of the artichokes to remove the tough leaf bases. Quarter the artichokes and remove the hairy chokes.
2. Add 3 tablespoons of the lemon juice to a pan of boiling salted water. Add the artichoke hearts and cook for 20–25 minutes, until tender. Drain and cool quickly under running cold water. Drain well, pat dry with kitchen paper and place in a bowl.
3. Mix together the remaining lemon juice, olive oil, herbs, and salt and pepper. Pour over the artichokes and stir well. Chill for 1–2 hours, if possible.
4. Arrange the salami and artichoke hearts on 4 individual plates and garnish with lemon slices to serve.

ARTICHOKES WITH MARINATED MUSHROOMS AND PARMA HAM

Make this starter up to a day in advance if necessary; keep the artichokes and filling separate until serving time.

4 globe artichokes
5 tablespoons wine
  vinegar
3 tablespoons lemon juice
6 tablespoons olive oil
1 tablespoon chopped
  parsley

2 teaspoons Dijon mustard
125 g (4 oz) button
  mushrooms, sliced thinly
50 g (2 oz) Parma ham,
  cut into thin strips
salt and pepper to taste

1. Trim the stalks from the artichokes and remove any tough leaves from the base; wash well. Bring a large pan of water to the boil, add the vinegar and artichokes, cover and cook for about 35 minutes, until a leaf can be pulled out easily. Drain upside down in a colander and leave to cool.

2. Whisk the lemon juice, oil, parsley, mustard, and salt and pepper together until thick. Place the mushrooms and ham in a small bowl, pour over the dressing and toss well. Leave to marinate for at least 1 hour.

3. Open out the leaves from each artichoke and carefully remove the hairy choke with a teaspoon. Place the artichokes on 4 individual plates and fill the centres with the mushroom mixture.

Serves 4
Preparation time:
30 minutes, plus marinating
Cooking time:
About 35 minutes
Freezing:
Not recommended

VEGETABLES WITH GREEN SAUCE

This sharp-tasting green sauce provides a lively dip for all kinds of summer vegetables.

*750 g–1 kg (1½–2 lb)
    fresh summer vegetables,
    e.g. courgettes, fennel,
    peppers, carrots, cherry
    tomatoes, lettuce hearts,
    spring onions,
    mangetouts
FOR THE SAUCE:
1 clove garlic, crushed*

*1 tablespoon capers,
    chopped finely
3 tablespoons chopped
    parsley
1 tablespoon wine vinegar
1 teaspoon Dijon mustard
6 tablespoons olive oil
salt and pepper to taste*

Serves 4–6
Preparation time:
30 minutes
Freezing:
Not recommended

1. First prepare the sauce. Mix together the garlic, capers, parsley, vinegar and mustard. Stir in the oil a little at a time, then season with salt and pepper. Place in a small bowl.
2. Cut the vegetables into large chunks, or leave whole if small. Arrange in a large bowl or basket, or on 4–6 individual plates, and serve with the green sauce for dipping.

VEGETABLES WITH MUSTARD MAYONNAISE

Adapt the recipe to each season, choosing the freshest, most colourful vegetables available which offer a variety of textures and flavours.

*1 red pepper, cored and
    seeded
2–3 courgettes
2–3 carrots
½ cauliflower
125 g (4 oz) button
    mushrooms*

*1 bunch radishes
5 tablespoons mayonnaise
2 teaspoons wine vinegar
1 tablespoon olive oil
1 teaspoon coarse grain
    mustard
salt and pepper to taste*

Serves 4
Preparation time:
25 minutes
Freezing:
Not recommended

1. Have ready a bowl of iced water if you are preparing the vegetables in advance. Cut the pepper into strips. Cut the courgettes and carrots into sticks. Break the cauliflower into small florets. Place all the vegetables in the iced water if necessary.
2. Mix the remaining ingredients together and place in a small bowl set on a large platter.
3. Drain the vegetables thoroughly if necessary and arrange in piles around the edge of the platter.

PROVENCE-STYLE GREEN BEANS

500 g (1 lb) French beans
2 tablespoons olive oil
2 cloves garlic, chopped
finely

2 tomatoes, skinned and
chopped
salt and pepper to taste

1. Cook the beans in boiling salted water for about 10 minutes, until just tender. Drain well and set aside.
2. Heat the oil in a saucepan, add the garlic, and salt and pepper and fry gently for 2 minutes. Add the tomatoes and cook for 2–3 minutes, until they become slightly pulpy. Add the beans, stirring well, cover and cook for 3–4 minutes.
3. Divide between 4 individual warmed plates and serve piping hot, with French bread to mop up the juices.

Serves 4
Preparation time:
15 minutes
Cooking time:
About 20 minutes
Freezing:
Not recommended

ASPARAGUS WITH CREAM AND ALMONDS

Asparagus, with its all too short season, is a rare luxury. A topping of seasoned cream and sweet almonds pushes it right over the top!

500 g (1 lb) asparagus
142 ml (5 fl oz) carton
   double cream
1 tablespoon lemon juice

25 g (1 oz) flaked
   almonds, toasted
salt and pepper to taste

Serves 4
Preparation time:
15 minutes
Cooking time:
12–15 minutes
Freezing:
Not recommended

1. Bend the asparagus spears until they snap. Discard the tough ends, or peel and use to make soup. Boil or steam the asparagus spears for 12–15 minutes, until tender.
2. Whip the cream until fairly stiff. Fold in half of the lemon juice and season with salt and pepper.
3. Arrange the asparagus on 4 individual warmed plates. Sprinkle over the remaining lemon juice, then top with a spoonful of cream. Sprinkle with the almonds and serve immediately.

ASPARAGUS AND EGG TARTS

When asparagus is out of season, use lightly cooked green beans, broccoli or spinach. Use sifted plain white flour or plain wholemeal flour for the pastry, according to taste.

175 g (6 oz) shortcrust
   pastry (see Country
   Garden Tarts, page 64)
175 g (6 oz) asparagus,
   cooked

4 eggs
4 teaspoons single cream
4 teaspoons grated
   Parmesan cheese

Serves 4
Preparation time:
20 minutes, plus
making pastry
Cooking time:
30–35 minutes
Freezing:
Not recommended

1. Roll out the pastry on a floured surface and use to line four 10 cm (4 inch) flan tins. Line with greaseproof paper, fill with baking beans or rice and bake blind in a preheated oven, 200°C/400°F/Gas Mark 6, for 10 minutes. Remove the paper and beans and return to the oven for 5 minutes, until browned. Lower the temperature to 180°C/350°F/Gas Mark 4.
2. Curl the asparagus around the inside edge of each flan case. Break an egg into the centre of each, then top with a teaspoon each of cream and Parmesan cheese.
3. Return the tarts to the oven for 15–20 minutes, until the egg has just set. Serve warm.

GINGERED KING PRAWNS

You can cook these prawns on the barbecue as part of an
outdoor meal—when the weather obliges!

12 uncooked king prawns
2 tablespoons sunflower
* oil*
3 tablespoons lemon juice
1 onion, grated
2 cloves garlic, crushed

2 teaspoons grated fresh
* root ginger*
1/2 teaspoon chilli powder
salt and pepper to taste
lemon slices and parsley
* sprigs to garnish*

Serves 4
Preparation time:
25 minutes, plus
marinating
Cooking time:
5–6 minutes
Freezing:
Not recommended

1. Peel the prawns, leaving on the tail ends. Slit along the
back to remove the black digestive tract. Thread the
prawns onto 4 bamboo skewers.
2. Mix together the remaining ingredients, brush all over
the prawns and leave to marinate for 1 hour, occasionally
brushing with more mixture.
3. Cook the prawns under a preheated medium grill for
5–6 minutes, turning once, until they are pink and lightly
browned. Garnish with lemon and parsley to serve.

SASHIMI

Use only perfectly fresh fish for this raw fish dish.

1 salmon steak or salmon
* trout, weighing about*
* 250 g (8 oz)*
175 g (6 oz) firm white fish,
* e.g. bass, turbot, halibut*
125 g (4 oz) white radish
* (mooli), grated*

1 carrot, grated
1 small turnip, grated
1 tablespoon Japanese
* horseradish (wasabi)*
150 ml (1/4 pint) Japanese
* soy sauce*

Serves 4
Preparation time:
25–30 minutes,
plus chilling
Freezing:
Not recommended

1. Remove the skin and bones from all the fish. Using a
very sharp knife, cut the fish into wafer-thin slices and
arrange attractively on 4 individual plates.
2. Place piles of radish, and carrot and turnip on each
plate, cover and chill for 1 hour.
3. Blend the wasabi to a smooth paste with water and
place a little on each plate. Divide the soy sauce between 4
tiny bowls and place beside the plates.
4. To serve, diners dip their slivers of fish first into the
wasabi, then the soy sauce.

SMOKED TROUT PURÉE WITH FRESH TOMATO SAUCE

Smoked trout can be bought already filleted, or as whole fish. If you buy whole fish you will need about 400 g (14 oz). Carefully remove the skin and bones before using.

*250 g (8 oz) smoked trout
    fillets, chopped
1 tablespoon lemon juice
1 teaspoon grated lemon
    rind
pinch of cayenne pepper*

*75 g (3 oz) Greek strained
    yogurt
1 teaspoon chopped dill
250 g (8 oz) ripe tomatoes,
    skinned and seeded
salt and pepper to taste
dill sprigs to garnish*

Serves 4
Preparation time:
25 minutes, plus
chilling
Freezing:
Recommended

1. Place the trout, lemon juice and rind, cayenne, yogurt, dill, and salt and pepper in a blender or food processor and work together until smooth. Place in a bowl and chill for 1 hour.
2. Purée the tomatoes, seasoned with salt and pepper, in the blender or food processor.
3. To serve, place a spoonful of tomato sauce on 4 individual plates. Place spoonfuls of smoked trout purée on top and garnish with dill. Serve with fingers or triangles of wholemeal toast.

SMOKED SALMON WHIRLS

These morsels of smoked salmon wrapped around a creamy filling make an elegant starter for a summer meal.

*175 g (6 oz) smoked
    salmon
113 g (4 oz) carton curd
    cheese
1 teaspoon lemon juice*

*2 tablespoons snipped
    chives
black pepper to taste
1 carton mustard and
    cress to garnish*

Serves 4
Preparation time:
10 minutes, plus
chilling
Freezing:
Not recommended

1. Place the salmon on a board, overlapping the slices to make 2 rough oblongs about 15 × 10 cm (6 × 4 inches).
2. Beat together the cheese, lemon juice, chives and pepper and spread carefully over the salmon. Roll up each oblong carefully from one long edge, place on a plate and chill for 1 hour, until firm.
3. Using a sharp knife, cut the rolls into thin slices and arrange in a circle on 4 individual plates. Garnish with little bundles of mustard and cress.

HERBED YOGURT CHEESE

Natural yogurt makes a delightful fresh tasty soft cheese, perfect for summer days. Start the preparations the day before required.

450 g (1 lb) carton natural yogurt
½ teaspoon salt
2 tablespoons chopped herbs, e.g. chives, parsley, basil, oregano, tarragon
pepper to taste

tarragon sprigs to garnish
TO SERVE:
2 tablespoons olive oil
1 clove garlic, crushed
8–12 slices French bread
2 bunches radishes

Serves 4
Preparation time:
20 minutes, plus draining time
Freezing:
Not recommended

1. Line a sieve with muslin or a clean fine tea towel and place over a bowl.
2. Mix together the yogurt and salt, pour into the sieve and leave to drain for 12 hours, or overnight.
3. Turn the yogurt cheese into a bowl and mix with the herbs and pepper.
4. Mix together the oil and garlic. Toast the bread on one side. Brush the untoasted side with the garlic oil, then toast until brown and crisp.
5. Garnish the yogurt cheese with tarragon and serve with the radishes and garlic toast.

LETTUCE AND CHERVIL SOUP

1 large cos lettuce, shredded
600 ml (1 pint) hot chicken stock*
bunch of chervil
600 ml (1 pint) milk

pinch of grated nutmeg
1 tablespoon lemon juice
salt and pepper to taste
4–6 thin slices lemon to garnish

Serves 4–6
Preparation time:
20 minutes
Cooking time:
15 minutes
Freezing:
Not recommended

1. Place the lettuce, stock, chervil, and salt and pepper in a large pan. Bring to the boil, then cover and simmer for 10 minutes, until the lettuce is tender. Purée in a blender or food processor.
2. Return the soup to the pan, add the milk and nutmeg and heat gently. Check the seasoning.
3. Just before serving, stir in the lemon juice. Pour into individual warmed soup plates and float a slice of lemon on top of each serving.

WEST COUNTRY HERB SOUP

The wonderful flavour of fresh herbs is delightfully refreshing in this classy summer soup.

25 g (1 oz) butter
1 large onion, chopped
1 leek, sliced
500 g (1 lb) spinach, chopped
1 potato, chopped
1 tablespoon each chopped parsley, mint and chives

2 teaspoons chopped thyme
1.2 litres (2 pints) vegetable stock*
142 ml (5 fl oz) carton single cream
salt and pepper to taste
parsley sprigs to garnish

Serves 4
Preparation time:
25 minutes
Cooking time:
15–20 minutes
Freezing:
Not recommended

1. Melt the butter in a large saucepan, add the onion and leek and fry gently until softened. Add the spinach, potato, herbs and stock. Bring to the boil, then cover and simmer for 15–20 minutes, until the potato is tender.
2. Purée the soup in a blender or food processor. Return to the pan, add the cream, and salt and pepper and reheat gently. Serve hot, garnished with parsley.

WATERCRESS AND LEEK SOUP

To serve chilled, use 2 tablespoons oil in place of butter.

25 g (1 oz) butter
1 leek, sliced thinly
2 bunches watercress, chopped
900 ml (1½ pints) hot vegetable stock*
strip of orange rind

3 tablespoons freshly squeezed orange juice
2 teaspoons cornflour, blended with 3 table-spoons single cream
salt and pepper to taste
shredded orange rind to garnish

Serves 4
Preparation time:
20 minutes
Cooking time:
8–10 minutes
Freezing:
Recommended, at end of stage 2

1. Melt the butter in a saucepan, add the leek and fry gently until softened. Add the watercress and stir until slightly wilted.
2. Add the hot stock and bring to the boil. Add the orange rind and juice, and salt and pepper, cover and simmer for 5 minutes, then purée in a blender or food processor until fairly smooth.
3. Return the soup to the pan, stir in the blended cornflour and cook until slightly thickened and smooth.
4. Serve hot or cold, garnished with orange rind and accompanied by Cheese Sticks* or small cheese biscuits.

CHILLED TOMATO AND BASIL SOUP

Tomato and basil are natural partners and taste particularly good in this refreshing summer soup. Make it the day before required, if you wish.

1 tablespoon oil
1 onion, chopped
1 potato, chopped
500 g (1 lb) tomatoes,
　skinned and quartered
2 tablespoons tomato
　purée

10 basil leaves
300 ml (½ pint) vegetable
　stock*
150 g (5.3 oz) carton
　natural set yogurt
salt and pepper to taste
snipped chives to garnish

Serves 4
Preparation time:
15 minutes, plus
chilling
Cooking time:
20 minutes
Freezing:
Recommended

1. Heat the oil in a pan, add the onion and fry until softened. Add the potato and stir well. Add the tomatoes, tomato purée, basil, stock, and salt and pepper, bring to the boil, then cover and simmer for 20 minutes.
2. Purée the soup in a blender or food processor, then stir in half of the yogurt. Leave to cool, then chill for at least 2 hours.
3. Transfer the soup to 4 individual bowls. Top with a spoonful of the remaining yogurt and a sprinkling of snipped chives to serve.

CHILLED CATALAN SOUP

This soup is similar to gazpacho, but with less tomato and more green vegetables. Ground almonds are added to thicken the soup slightly and add to the flavours.

1 Spanish onion, chopped
1 green pepper, cored, seeded and chopped
2 cloves garlic, crushed
¹/₂ cucumber, chopped
250 g (8 oz) ripe tomatoes, skinned and chopped
25 g (1 oz) ground almonds
1 tablespoon chopped parsley
2 tablespoons chopped mint
2 tablespoons olive oil
3 tablespoons wine vinegar
600 ml (1 pint) water
salt and pepper to taste
TO SERVE:
ice cubes
stuffed olives, sliced

1. Place all the ingredients, except the water, and salt and pepper, in a blender or food processor and work together until finely chopped. Add the water, and salt and pepper and process again. Transfer to a bowl, cover and chill for 2–3 hours.
2. Serve in individual bowls with a few ice cubes and olive slices on top.

Serves 4
Preparation time: 30 minutes, plus chilling
Freezing: Not recommended

ITALIAN BAKED TOMATOES

4 beefsteak tomatoes
25 g (1 oz) breadcrumbs,
  toasted
1 tablespoon chopped
  mixed herbs, e.g.
  tarragon, mint, chives
  and parsley

125 g (4 oz) mushrooms,
  chopped
25 g (1 oz) Parmesan
  cheese, grated
salt and pepper to taste
frisé or curly endive and
  parsley sprigs to garnish

Serves 4
Preparation time:
20 minutes
Cooking time:
15 minutes
Freezing:
Not recommended

1. Cut the tops off the tomatoes and scoop out the flesh into a sieve placed over a bowl. Sprinkle the insides of the tomatoes with salt and place upside down.
2. Press the tomato flesh through the sieve. Stir in the breadcrumbs, herbs, mushrooms, and salt and pepper.
3. Place the tomatoes in an oiled baking dish, fill with the mushroom mixture and sprinkle with the cheese. Bake in a preheated oven, 190°C/375°F/Gas Mark 5, for 15 minutes, until the tomatoes are tender. Serve warm or cold, garnished with frisé or curly endive and parsley.

GARLIC-BAKED PEPPERS WITH OLIVES

Try to get three different coloured peppers if possible as they look stunning on the plate. The peppers are baked for a short time to bring out their sweet flavour while retaining a delicious crunchy texture.

1 each red, green and
  yellow pepper,
  quartered, cored and
  seeded
2 cloves garlic, chopped
  finely

2 tomatoes, skinned and
  chopped finely
1 teaspoon capers,
  chopped
12 black olives
2 tablespoons olive oil
salt and pepper to taste

Serves 4
Preparation time:
15 minutes
Cooking time:
25 minutes
Freezing:
Not recommended

1. Place the peppers skin side down in a greased baking dish. Mix together the garlic, tomatoes, capers, and salt and pepper and spoon a little into each pepper quarter. Top each with an olive and drizzle over the oil.
2. Bake in a preheated oven, 190°C/375°F/Gas Mark 5, for 25 minutes. Serve warm or cold.

CELERIAC WITH EGG AND TARRAGON DRESSING

*1 head celeriac, weighing
  about 500 g (1 lb)*
1 tablespoon lemon juice
2 egg yolks
*1 tablespoon tarragon
  vinegar*
*1 tablespoon Dijon
  mustard*

2 tablespoons olive oil
*2 tablespoons soured
  cream*
salt and pepper to taste
*2 teaspoons chopped
  tarragon to garnish*

Serves 4
Preparation time:
20 minutes
Freezing:
Not recommended

1. Peel the celeriac thickly. Slice it thinly, then cut each slice into matchstick pieces. Place in a bowl with the lemon juice and mix well.
2. Beat together the egg yolks, vinegar, mustard, and salt and pepper, then gradually add the oil and soured cream. Add to the celeriac and mix well.
3. Pile the celeriac onto 4 individual plates and sprinkle with chopped tarragon. Serve as soon as possible.

AUBERGINE AND TAHINI PURÉE

Tahini is ground sesame paste. It has a warm subtle flavour which goes well with lightly spiced aubergine.

500 g (1 lb) aubergines
1 clove garlic
1 teaspoon salt
3 tablespoons tahini
5 tablespoons lemon juice
1/2 teaspoon chilli powder
1 teaspoon ground cumin

TO SERVE:
1 tablespoon olive oil
*1 tablespoon chopped
  parsley*
few black olives
pitta bread
lemon wedges

Serves 4
Preparation time:
10 minutes, plus
cooling
Cooking time:
25–30 minutes
Freezing:
Recommended

1. Make 3 long slits in each aubergine, place on a baking sheet and bake in a preheated oven, 220°C/425°F/Gas Mark 7, for 25–30 minutes, until the flesh feels soft. Leave until cool enough to handle.
2. Cut the aubergines in half and scoop out the flesh. Place in a blender or food processor with the garlic and salt and work together until smooth. Add the remaining ingredients and blend well. Transfer to a small bowl and leave to cool.
3. Just before serving, drizzle over the oil, sprinkle with the parsley and top with a few olives. Serve with triangles of warm pitta bread and lemon wedges.

PAKORAS WITH MINT CHUTNEY

Pakora batter is usually made with chick pea flour, which is very hard to find. Semolina works equally well and gives the fritters the same golden colour.

125 g (4 oz) semolina
1 teaspoon salt
½ teaspoon chilli powder
1 teaspoon turmeric
1 teaspoon garam masala
2 tablespoons natural
  yogurt
175 ml (6 fl oz) water
500 g (1 lb) vegetables, e.g.
  cauliflower, aubergines,
  courgettes, peppers,
  mushrooms
oil for deep-frying

mint sprigs to garnish
FOR THE CHUTNEY:
6 tablespoons chopped
  mint
1 small onion, chopped
  finely
1 teaspoon chilli powder
4 tablespoons natural
  yogurt
2 teaspoons clear honey
2 tablespoons vinegar
salt and pepper to taste

Serves 4
Preparation time:
30 minutes, plus
standing time
Cooking time:
2–3 minutes per
batch
Freezing:
Not recommended

1. Mix together the semolina, salt and spices in a bowl. Make a well in the centre and add the yogurt. Beat with a wooden spoon, gradually adding the water, to make a smooth batter. Leave to rest for 10 minutes.
2. Mix together the chutney ingredients and place in a small bowl. Cover and chill until required.
3. Prepare the vegetables: break the cauliflower into small florets, dice the aubergines, slice the courgettes, cut the peppers into strips; slice the mushrooms if large or leave whole if small. Add to the batter and stir to coat well.
4. Heat the oil in a large saucepan and deep-fry the vegetables in batches for 2–3 minutes, until crisp and golden. Drain well on kitchen paper and keep warm.
5. Garnish the pakoras with mint sprigs and serve hot with the chutney as a dipping sauce.

HOT GARLIC MUSHROOMS

These delicious mushrooms can be prepared in advance, ready to go in the oven.

4 small slices wholemeal
  bread
50 g (2 oz) butter
1 clove garlic, crushed
4 teaspoons lemon juice

500 g (1 lb) cup
  mushrooms, stalks
  removed
salt and pepper to taste

1. Butter 4 ramekins or other small ovenproof dishes. Cut the bread into rounds the same diameter as the dishes.

2. Beat together the butter, garlic, and salt and pepper. Spread a little on each slice of bread and place buttered side up in the dishes.

3. Pile the mushrooms into the dishes and spread the remaining garlic butter on top. Sprinkle with the lemon juice, and salt and pepper.

4. Cover with foil and bake in a preheated oven, 220°C/425°F/Gas Mark 7, for 25 minutes, until tender. Serve piping hot.

Serves 4
Preparation time:
15 minutes
Cooking time:
25 minutes
Freezing:
Not recommended

TAGLIATELLE WITH PECAN AND PARSLEY SAUCE

Use a mixture of green and white tagliatelle, if possible.

75 g (3 oz) shelled pecans
15 g (½ oz) parsley
25 g (1 oz) butter, softened
3 tablespoons grated Parmesan cheese
150 ml (¼ pint) olive oil

2 tablespoons natural fromage frais
250 g (12 oz) fresh tagliatelle or noodles
salt and pepper to taste

Serves 4
Preparation time:
20 minutes
Cooking time:
6–8 minutes
Freezing:
Not recommended

1. Place 50 g (2 oz) of the pecans and the parsley in a food processor or blender and work together until finely ground. Add the butter and Parmesan cheese and blend to mix well. Add the oil, a little at a time, and blend until the sauce is smooth and thick. Stir in the fromage frais and season with salt and pepper.
2. Cook the tagliatelle according to packet instructions. Drain well, then return to the pan with the sauce and heat gently, stirring to mix.
3. Transfer to 4 warmed individual plates. Roughly chop the remaining pecans and sprinkle over the pasta. Serve immediately.

GREEN GNOCCHI WITH TOMATO SAUCE

If you like, the gnocchi can be prepared, but not cooked, well in advance, and the sauce made ready for reheating.

500 g (1 lb) spinach
25 g (1 oz) butter or margarine
1 shallot, chopped finely
113 g (4 oz) carton curd cheese
2 egg yolks
75 g (3 oz) plain flour
50 g (2 oz) Parmesan cheese, grated

grated nutmeg
salt and pepper to taste
FOR THE SAUCE:
350 g (12 oz) ripe tomatoes, skinned and chopped
1 tablespoon tomato purée
pinch of sugar
2 tablespoons double cream

1. Place the spinach, with just the water clinging to the leaves after washing, in a large pan and cook for about 5 minutes, until tender. Drain well, pressing out as much water as possible, then chop finely. Place in a bowl.

2. Melt the butter or margarine in a small pan, add the shallot and fry until softened. Add to the spinach with the curd cheese, and salt and pepper. Mix well, then work in the egg yolks, flour, Parmesan cheese and a sprinkling of nutmeg. Cover and chill for at least 30 minutes, until firm.

3. Meanwhile, prepare the sauce. Place the tomatoes, tomato purée and sugar in a small pan. Heat gently until the tomatoes become more liquid, bring to the boil, then simmer for 10 minutes. Press through a sieve, return to the pan, add the cream and heat gently while cooking the gnocchi.

4. Have ready a pan of salted simmering water. Shape the gnocchi into 2 cm (¾ inch) balls. Add half to the pan and cook for about 5 minutes, or until they rise to the surface of the water. Remove with a slotted spoon and keep warm while you cook the rest.

5. Divide the gnocchi between 4 individual warmed dishes and pour over the tomato sauce to serve.

Serves 4
Preparation time: 45 minutes, plus chilling
Cooking time: About 5 minutes per batch
Freezing: Not recommended

CHICKEN LIVER AND SAGE CROSTINI

2 tablespoons olive oil
1 shallot, chopped
1 clove garlic, crushed
250 g (8 oz) chicken livers,
*   chopped*
50 g (2 oz) button
*   mushrooms, halved*
8 small sage leaves

4 tablespoons dry white
*   wine*
salt and pepper to taste
TO SERVE:
4 slices French bread, cut
*   diagonally, fried in oil*
sage leaves to garnish

Serves 4
Preparation time:
15 minutes
Cooking time:
10 minutes
Freezing:
Not recommended

1. Heat the oil in a frying pan, add the shallot and garlic and fry until softened.
2. Increase the heat, add the chicken livers and cook, stirring, until evenly coloured. Stir in the mushrooms and sage and cook for 1 minute.
3. Add the wine, and salt and pepper and cook for 2–3 minutes, until the livers are cooked but still pink inside.
4. Arrange the fried bread on 4 warmed individual plates, pile the chicken liver mixture on top and garnish with the sage leaves. Serve hot.

GRILLED GREEK CHEESE PARCELS

A simple starter, but one which is sure to be a great success—the slightly sharp tasting vine leaves go so well with the creamy melting cheese.

¹/₂ packet vine leaves
350 g (12 oz) Haloumi
*   cheese, cut into small*
*   squares*

TO SERVE:
few vine leaves (optional)
lemon slices

Serves 4
Preparation time:
10 minutes, plus
soaking time
Cooking time:
5 minutes
Freezing:
Not recommended

1. Separate the vine leaves and place in a bowl. Pour over boiling water and leave to soak for 20 minutes. Drain and place in a bowl with cold water to cover for 10 minutes. Drain well and dry with kitchen paper.
2. Wrap each piece of cheese in a vine leaf, securing with wooden cocktail sticks if necessary. Cook under a pre-heated hot grill for 5 minutes, until the cheese has melted.
3. Remove the cocktail sticks, if used, and serve the parcels on vine leaves if you wish, garnished with lemon slices.

SEASHELLS

125 g (4 oz) plain flour,
  sifted
1 teaspoon mustard
  powder (preferably
  coarse grain)
50 g (2 oz) Cheddar
  cheese, grated
50 g (2 oz) butter or
  margarine
1 tablespoon water
125 g (4 oz) peeled prawns
  (thawed if frozen)

125 g (4 oz) fresh or
  canned crab meat,
  drained and flaked
1 egg, beaten
142 ml (5 fl oz) carton
  single cream
1 tablespoon snipped
  chives
salt and pepper to taste
parsley sprigs to garnish

Serves 4
Preparation time:
20 minutes
Cooking time:
30–35 minutes
Freezing:
Recommended

1. Mix together the flour, mustard, half of the cheese, and salt and pepper. Rub in the butter or margarine until the mixture resembles breadcrumbs. Stir in the water and mix to a firm dough. Knead lightly.
2. Divide the dough into 4 pieces, then roll out to line 4 scallop shells. Trim the edges and prick the base.
3. Bake in a preheated oven, 200°C/400°F/Gas Mark 6, for 15 minutes, until golden brown. Lower the temperature to 180°C/350°F/Gas Mark 4.
4. Fill the pastry cases with the prawns and crab. Beat together the egg, cream, chives, and salt and pepper. Pour into the shells and sprinkle with the remaining cheese. Return to the oven for 15–20 minutes, until the filling is just firm. Serve hot, garnished with parsley.

HOT GRILLED AVOCADO

2 large ripe avocados,
  halved and stoned
175 g (6 oz) fresh or
  canned crab meat,
  drained
3 tablespoons single cream

1/2 teaspoon paprika
2 tablespoons wholemeal
  breadcrumbs
50 g (2 oz) Gruyère cheese,
  grated
salt to taste

Serves 4
Preparation time:
10–15 minutes
Cooking time:
3–4 minutes
Freezing:
Not recommended

1. Place the avocados cut side up in an ovenproof dish. Mix together the crab, cream, paprika and a little salt, then pile into the avocados.
2. Mix together the breadcrumbs and cheese and sprinkle over the avocados. Place under a preheated hot grill for 3–4 minutes, until the topping is crisp and golden brown. Serve immediately.

SMOKED HADDOCK SOUP

This soup is a slight variation of a traditional Scottish one called Cullen Skink. I sometimes add a few peas or skinned and chopped tomatoes for extra colour.

500 g (1 lb) smoked
* haddock*
600 ml (1 pint) milk
300 ml (½ pint) water
25 g (1 oz) butter
1 tablespoon oil
1 onion, chopped finely

350 g (12 oz) floury
* potatoes, diced*
2 tablespoons chopped
* parsley*
grated nutmeg and pepper
* to taste*

Serves 4
Preparation time:
30 minutes
Cooking time:
About 20 minutes
Freezing:
Recommended

1. Place the haddock, milk and water in a saucepan, bring to the boil, then cover and simmer for 10 minutes, until the fish flakes easily. Carefully transfer with a fish slice to a plate and leave to cool slightly. Strain the cooking liquid and set aside.
2. Heat the butter and oil in the saucepan, add the onion and fry until softened. Add the potatoes and cook for 5 minutes. Add the reserved cooking liquid, bring to the boil, then cover and simmer for about 20 minutes, until the potato has broken down; mash it if necessary.
3. Skin and flake the fish and add to the soup with the nutmeg, pepper and parsley. Heat gently for 5 minutes. Serve with wholemeal bread.

LEMON SOLE BAKED IN A PAPER CASE

Allow each diner to open his or her own parcel—the aroma that escapes is almost as good as the taste.

1 small bulb fennel
1 tablespoon oil
1 shallot, chopped
1 leek, shredded
4 tomatoes, skinned,
* seeded and chopped*

4 lemon sole fillets, each
* weighing about 125 g*
* (4 oz)*
salt and pepper to taste

1. Remove the feathery leaves from the fennel and re-serve. Cut the bulb into fine julienne strips.
2. Heat the oil in a small pan, add the shallot and fry over high heat for 1 minute. Lower the heat, add the leek and fennel and fry for 5 minutes. Add the tomatoes, and salt and pepper and simmer for 5 minutes.

3. Cut out 4 heart-shaped pieces of greaseproof paper, twice the size of the fish, and brush with oil. Place the fish on one half, spoon over the sauce and sprinkle with the reserved fennel leaves. Fold the paper over to enclose the fish and seal well.
4. Place the parcels on 2 baking sheets and bake in a preheated oven, 200°C/400°F/Gas Mark 6, for 10 minutes. Serve the fish in the unopened parcels, placed on individual warmed plates.

Serves 4
Preparation time:
35 minutes
Cooking time:
10 minutes
Freezing:
Not recommended

STILTON, CELERY AND APPLE SOUP

25 g (1 oz) butter or margarine
1 onion, chopped finely
3 celery sticks, chopped finely
1 tablespoon plain flour
150 ml (1/4 pint) dry white wine
600 ml (1 pint) vegetable stock*

300 ml (1/2 pint) milk
1 bay leaf
1 cooking apple, peeled and chopped
75 g (3 oz) Stilton cheese
salt and pepper to taste
celery leaves to garnish

Serves 4
Preparation time:
25 minutes
Cooking time:
30 minutes
Freezing:
Recommended, at end of stage 2

1. Melt the butter or margarine in a large pan, add the onion and celery and fry gently until slightly softened. Stir in the flour and cook for 1 minute.
2. Gradually stir in the wine and stock and cook, stirring, until thickened and smooth. Add the milk, bay leaf, apple, and salt and pepper. Bring to the boil, then cover and simmer for 30 minutes.
3. Remove from the heat and discard the bay leaf. Crumble in the Stilton and stir until completely melted. Serve piping hot, garnished with celery leaves.

PUMPKIN SOUP

Pumpkin is usually inexpensive and plentiful in the autumn. It makes one of my favourite seasonal soups—rich, creamy and full of flavour.

2 tablespoons olive oil
1 large onion, chopped
1 clove garlic, crushed
125 g (4 oz) streaky bacon, derinded and chopped
1 kg (2 lb) pumpkin, peeled, seeded and chopped finely

1 potato, chopped finely
1 bouquet garni
900 ml (1 1/2 pints) vegetable stock*
432 g (15 1/4 oz) can borlotti beans, drained
salt and pepper to taste

Serves 4–6
Preparation time:
35 minutes
Cooking time:
1 hour 10 minutes
Freezing:
Recommended

1. Heat the oil in a large saucepan, add the onion and garlic and fry until softened. Add the bacon and fry for 5 minutes.
2. Add the pumpkin, potato, bouquet garni, stock, and salt and pepper. Bring to the boil, then cover and simmer for 1 hour, until the vegetables are very tender.
3. Stir in the beans and simmer for 10 minutes. Serve hot.

INDONESIAN CHICKEN SOUP

Even those who are less inclined to spicy foods will enjoy
this light, sweet-tasting soup.

*125 g (4 oz) boneless
  chicken breast, skinned
  and sliced thinly*
1/2 teaspoon turmeric
1/2 teaspoon chilli powder
1 tablespoon sunflower oil
*3 tablespoons chopped
  spring onions*
*75 g (3 oz) creamed
  coconut, grated and
  blended with 450 ml
  (3/4 pint) boiling water*
*300 ml (1/2 pint) chicken
  stock**

2 tablespoons lime juice
*1 teaspoon light brown soft
  sugar*
50 g (2 oz) long-grain rice
*1 tablespoon crunchy
  peanut butter*
*75 g (3 oz) canned
  waterchestnuts, sliced
  thinly*
salt and pepper to taste
*chopped spring onion tops
  to garnish*

Serves 4
Preparation time:
20 minutes
Cooking time:
12–15 minutes
Freezing:
Recommended

1. Place the chicken, turmeric and chilli in a bowl and mix
well.
2. Heat the oil in a large saucepan, add the chicken and
stir-fry quickly for about 2 minutes, until browned. Stir in
the spring onions.
3. Add the blended coconut, stock, lime juice, sugar, rice
and peanut butter. Bring to the boil, then cover and
simmer for 12–15 minutes, until the rice is cooked.
4. Add the waterchestnuts, and salt and pepper and heat
gently. Pour into 4 individual warmed soup bowls and
sprinkle with chopped spring onion tops to serve.

RED ONION SOUP

This soup is similar to the well loved French onion. The
red onions give it a particularly good flavour and colour.

25 g (1 oz) butter
1 tablespoon oil
*500 g (1 lb) red onions,
  sliced thinly*
1/2 teaspoon sugar
*2 × 298 g (10½ oz) cans
  concentrated
  consommé*
2 tablespoons sherry

pepper to taste
TO SERVE:
*4 small slices wholemeal
  bread, toasted*
*4 teaspoons coarse grain
  mustard*
*25 g (1 oz) Gruyère cheese,
  grated*

1. Melt the butter and oil in a large saucepan, add the onions and fry gently until softened. Add the sugar and cook for 10 minutes.

2. Add the consommé with 2 cans of water, bring to the boil, then cover and simmer for 30 minutes. Add the sherry and simmer for 5 minutes. Season with pepper.

3. Spread the toast with the mustard, cut each slice into quarters and place in 4 individual warmed soup bowls, mustard side up. Pour over the soup and sprinkle with the cheese to serve.

Serves 4
Preparation time:
25 minutes
Cooking time:
45 minutes
Freezing:
Not recommended

FRIED POTATO SKINS

For a casual party, these crispy slivers can be handed around with the welcoming drinks. They are great for working up an appetite. Use the potatoes for another dish.

1.5 kg (3 lb) old potatoes
142 ml (5 fl oz) carton
*   soured cream*

1 teaspoon paprika
oil for deep-frying .
sea salt and pepper to taste

Serves 4
Preparation time:
15 minutes
Cooking time:
3–4 minutes per batch
Freezing:
Not recommended

1. Peel the potatoes into strips, taking a little potato with the skin. Pat dry with kitchen paper.
2. Mix together the soured cream, paprika and pepper and place in a small dish.
3. Heat the oil to 180°C/350°F, or until a potato skin rises instantly to the surface when added. Fry the skins in two batches, until crisp and golden. Drain on kitchen paper. Sprinkle with sea salt and serve with the sauce for dipping.

STUFFED MUSHROOMS

350 g (12 oz) open
*   mushrooms*
2 tablespoons oil
2 shallots, chopped
1 clove garlic, crushed
125 g (4 oz) back bacon,
*   derinded and chopped*
*   finely*

1 teaspoon chopped
*   rosemary*
25 g (1 oz) walnuts,
*   chopped finely*
50 g (2 oz) wholemeal
*   breadcrumbs*
50 g (2 oz) Cheddar
*   cheese, grated*
salt and pepper to taste

Serves 4
Preparation time:
30 minutes
Cooking time:
10–12 minutes
Freezing:
Not recommended

1. Remove the mushroom stalks and chop finely. Place the mushrooms, open side up, in a large oiled tin.
2. Heat the oil in a frying pan, add the shallots and garlic and fry until softened. Add the bacon and mushroom stalks and fry for 5 minutes.
3. Stir in the rosemary, walnuts, breadcrumbs, and salt and pepper and mix well. Pile a little of the mixture onto each mushroom, then sprinkle with the cheese.
4. Bake in a preheated oven, 200°C/400°F/Gas Mark 6, for 10–12 minutes, until the mushrooms are tender and the cheese has melted. Serve immediately.

STEAMED LEEK PARCELS

These light vegetable parcels with their creamy leek sauce are an ideal way to start a more substantial winter meal, such as a roast or hearty stew.

2 large leeks
3 carrots
3 celery sticks
25 g (1 oz) butter

1 teaspoon chopped mint
284 ml (10 fl oz) carton
single cream
salt and pepper to taste

Serves 4
Preparation time:
30 minutes
Cooking time:
20 minutes
Freezing:
Not recommended

1. Trim the leeks, then cut in half lengthways. Set aside 8 outside strips and finely chop the rest.
2. Cut the carrots and celery into matchstick pieces, about 6 cm (2½ inches) long. Make 8 bundles of carrot and celery sticks and wrap a strip of leek around each. Secure with wooden cocktail sticks.
3. Place the parcels on a heatproof plate with 1 tablespoon water. Cover tightly with foil, place over a pan of simmering water and steam for 20 minutes, until the vegetables are just tender.
4. Meanwhile, melt the butter in a small pan, add the chopped leeks and stir well. Cover and cook gently for 2–3 minutes. Add the mint, and salt and pepper and cook for 2 minutes. Stir in the cream, bring gently to simmering point and cook for 2–3 minutes. Purée in a blender or food processor, then return to the pan to keep warm.
5. Spread a pool of leek sauce on 4 individual warmed plates. Remove the cocktail sticks from the vegetables and place 2 parcels on each plate. Serve piping hot.

LENTIL-STUFFED VINE LEAVES

250 g (8 oz) packet vine
leaves in brine, drained
1 small onion, chopped
finely
125 g (4 oz) red lentils
300 ml (½ pint) water
½ teaspoon chilli powder
1 teaspoon garam masala
2 teaspoons tomato purée

25 g (1 oz) raisins
3 tablespoons lemon juice
salt and pepper to taste
TO SERVE:
250 g (8 oz) Greek
strained yogurt
1 clove garlic, crushed
1–2 tablespoons lemon
juice

1. Place the vine leaves in a bowl, cover with boiling water and leave for 20 minutes. Drain, cover with cold water, leave for another 20 minutes, then drain well.

2. Meanwhile place the onion, lentils, water, chilli powder, garam masala, tomato purée, raisins and 1 tablespoon of the lemon juice in a pan. Bring to the boil, then cover tightly and cook gently for about 20 minutes, until all the water is absorbed and the lentils are softened. Season with salt and pepper and leave to cool.

3. Place a teaspoonful of the mixture on each vine leaf and roll up like a parcel, tucking in the ends to enclose the filling completely.

4. Place the parcels in a large frying pan. Add the remaining lemon juice and 300 ml (½ pint) water. Bring to the boil, cover tightly and simmer for 30 minutes. Drain.

5. Serve warm or cold with the yogurt, flavoured with the garlic and lemon juice.

Serves 6–8
Preparation time:
40 minutes, plus
soaking time
Cooking time:
30 minutes
Freezing:
Recommended

COUNTRY GARDEN TARTS

Vegetarians in particular should enjoy these little whole-meal tarts packed with crisp vegetables. The Lancashire cheese can be replaced with vegetarian Cheddar.

*FOR THE SHORTCRUST
   PASTRY:
175 g (6 oz) plain
   wholemeal flour
pinch of salt
75 g (3 oz) butter or
   margarine, diced
2 tablespoons water
   (approximately)
FOR THE FILLING:
2 tablespoons oil
1 celery stick, chopped
   finely
1 leek, sliced thinly*

*125 g (4 oz) broccoli, cut
   into tiny florets
1 carrot, grated
1 egg
150 g (5.3 oz) carton
   natural yogurt
50 g (2 oz) Lancashire
   cheese, grated
1 tablespoon chopped
   parsley
salt and pepper to taste
TO SERVE:
frisé or curly endive
thinly sliced leek*

Serves 4
Preparation time:
40 minutes, plus chilling
Cooking time:
20 minutes
Freezing:
Recommended

1. To make the pastry, place the flour and salt in a large bowl and rub in the butter or margarine until the mixture resembles breadcrumbs. Mix in enough water to form a stiff dough.

2. Place on a lightly floured board and knead lightly until smooth. Wrap in foil and chill for 15 minutes.

3. Roll out on a lightly floured board and use to line four 10 cm (4 inch) flan tins. Line with greaseproof paper, fill with baking beans or rice and bake blind in a preheated oven, 200°C/400°F/Gas Mark 6, for 10 minutes. Remove the beans and paper and return to the oven for 5 minutes. Lower the temperature to 180°C/350°F/Gas Mark 4.

4. Meanwhile, prepare the filling. Heat the oil in a pan, add the celery, leek and broccoli and stir well. Lower the heat, cover the pan and allow the vegetables to sweat for 5 minutes. Add the carrot, and salt and pepper and cook for 5 minutes. Divide between the pastry cases.

5. Beat together the egg, yogurt, cheese, parsley, and salt and pepper, then pour over the vegetables. Return to the oven for 20 minutes, until the filling is firm and golden brown.

6. Carefully remove the flans from the tins and place on individual plates, lined with frisé or curly endive and a few leek rings. Serve warm.

SKEWERED SCALLOPS WITH BACON

When queen scallops are not available, use the larger ones
and cut into 2 or 3 pieces.

*350 g (12 oz) queen
    scallops
2 tablespoons lime juice
1 tablespoon sunflower oil
1 teaspoon dried dill*

*125 g (4 oz) streaky bacon,
    sliced thinly and
    derinded
salt and pepper to taste
lime wedges and parsley
    sprigs to serve*

Serves 4
Preparation time:
20 minutes, plus
marinating
Cooking time:
6–8 minutes
Freezing:
Not recommended

1. Place the scallops, lime juice, oil, dill, and salt and
pepper in a bowl, mix well, then leave to marinate for
1 hour, stirring occasionally.
2. Stretch the bacon with the back of a knife, then cut each
rasher into 3 pieces. Wrap each piece around a scallop and
thread onto 4 or 8 bamboo skewers.
3. Cook under a preheated moderate grill for 6–8
minutes, turning once, until the bacon is crisp and the
scallops are cooked. Serve hot, garnished with lime
wedges and parsley sprigs.

BAKED MUSSELS

Keep a bag of ready-cooked, frozen mussels in the freezer
to make this speedy starter when you're caught on the hop!

*50 g (2 oz) butter
1 clove garlic, crushed
1 tablespoon chopped
    parsley
2 teaspoons lemon juice*

*250 g (8 oz) cooked
    mussels (thawed if
    frozen)
125 g (4 oz) ready-made
    puff pastry
pepper to taste
beaten egg to glaze*

Serves 4
Preparation time:
15 minutes
Cooking time:
10–12 minutes
Freezing:
Not recommended

1. Beat together the butter, garlic, parsley, lemon juice
and pepper. Divide the mussels between 4 ramekin dishes
and spread the garlic butter over the top.
2. Roll out the pastry on a lightly floured surface and cut
into 4 rounds slightly larger than the ramekins. Dampen
the edges of the dishes, press the pastry on top and make a
hole in the centre. Brush with beaten egg.
3. Bake in a preheated oven, 220°C/425°F/Gas Mark 7, for
10–12 minutes, until the pastry is risen and golden brown.
Serve piping hot.

WARM CHICKEN LIVER SALAD

selection of salad leaves,
  e.g. frisé, radicchio,
  lettuce, watercress
2 tablespoons oil
1 shallot, sliced
250 g (8 oz) chicken livers,
  halved

125 g (4 oz) button
  mushrooms, sliced
2 tablespoons red wine
  vinegar
salt and pepper to taste

Serves 4
Preparation time:
15 minutes
Cooking time:
10–15 minutes
Freezing:
Not recommended

1. Tear the leaves into small pieces and arrange on 4 individual plates.
2. Heat the oil in a frying pan, add the shallot and fry until softened. Add the livers and fry quickly for about 5 minutes, until browned all over. Stir in the mushrooms and cook briefly, until just beginning to soften.
3. Remove from the pan with a slotted spoon and divide between the plates of salad.
4. Add the vinegar, and salt and pepper to the pan, stirring to scrape up any sediment. Bring to the boil, then quickly pour over the chicken livers. Serve immediately.

CHICKEN LIVER AND MUSHROOM PÂTÉ

250 g (8 oz) chicken livers
50 g (2 oz) butter
1 clove garlic, crushed
125 g (4 oz) mushrooms,
  chopped

1 tablespoon sherry
1 teaspoon chopped thyme
1 tablespoon each chopped
  parsley and chives
salt and pepper to taste

Serves 4
Preparation time:
15 minutes, plus
chilling
Cooking time:
10 minutes
Freezing:
Recommended

1. Trim off any dark patches from the chicken livers. Rinse and pat dry with kitchen paper.
2. Melt half of the butter in a frying pan, add the garlic and chicken livers and fry quickly on all sides for about 5 minutes, until evenly browned. Add the mushrooms, sherry, thyme, and salt and pepper and cook gently for 5 minutes.
3. Place in a blender or food processor and work until smooth. Transfer to a small dish, level the top and sprinkle with the parsley and chives.
4. Melt the remaining butter and pour evenly over the top. Leave until set, then chill for 1–2 hours until firm.
5. Remove from the refrigerator 30 minutes before required. Serve with fingers of wholemeal toast and a few salad leaves.

BARBECUED RIBS

1 kg (2 lb) pork spare ribs	*2 teaspoons English*
4 tablespoons clear honey	*mustard*
3 tablespoons pure orange	*3 tablespoons soy sauce*
juice	*3 tablespoons wine*
3 tablespoons tomato	*vinegar*
ketchup	*lemon slices to garnish*

1. Arrange the ribs in a single layer in the grill pan and cook under a preheated moderate grill for 12–15 minutes, turning once, until lightly browned and crisp. Drain on kitchen paper and place in a roasting tin.
2. Mix the remaining ingredients together until smooth, pour over the ribs and mix until well coated.
3. Bake in a preheated oven, 190°C/375°F/Gas Mark 5, for 30–35 minutes, turning occasionally, until tender. Serve piping hot, garnished with lemon slices.

Serves 4
Preparation time:
25 minutes
Cooking time:
30–35 minutes
Freezing:
Recommended

BAKED GOATS' CHEESE WITH SALAD

250 g (8 oz) chèvre (goats'
cheese), cut into 4 slices
olive oil for brushing
25 g (1 oz) wholemeal
breadcrumbs
2 teaspoons chopped sage
2 teaspoons snipped chives
FOR THE SALAD:
selection of salad leaves,
e.g. oak leaf lettuce,
frisé or curly endive,
corn salad, radicchio

6 radishes, sliced
50 g (2 oz) mushrooms,
sliced
FOR THE DRESSING:
1 tablespoon lemon juice
3 tablespoons olive oil
1/2 teaspoon clear honey
1 teaspoon Dijon mustard
salt and pepper to taste

Serves 4
Preparation time:
20 minutes
Cooking time:
12–15 minutes
Freezing:
Not recommended

1. Halve each slice of goats' cheese and brush all over with olive oil. Mix together the breadcrumbs, sage and chives and press onto the cheeses.
2. Place on a greased baking sheet and bake in a pre-heated oven, 200°C/400°F/Gas Mark 6, for 12–15 minutes, until the cheese has melted and the coating is crisp.
3. Meanwhile, prepare the salad. Divide the leaves between 4 individual dishes and sprinkle with the radishes and mushrooms.
4. Place the dressing ingredients in a screw-top jar and shake well to mix.
5. Place 2 pieces of hot goats' cheese on top of each salad and pour over the dressing. Serve immediately.

CAMEMBERT PUFF PIE WITH CRANBERRY AND PORT RELISH

Warm creamy Camembert in a crisp crust, served with a tangy cranberry sauce, provides a deliciously different winter starter. Use fresh or frozen cranberries.

200 g (7 oz) ready-made
puff pastry
270 g (9 oz) whole
Camembert
2 teaspoons green pepper-
corns, crushed lightly
beaten egg to glaze
FOR THE RELISH:
125 g (4 oz) cranberries

2 tablespoons freshly
squeezed orange juice
1/2 teaspoon grated orange
rind
5 tablespoons water
50 g (2 oz) light brown soft
sugar
1 tablespoon port

1. Roll out half of the pastry to a round slightly larger than the Camembert. Place the Camembert in the centre and sprinkle with the peppercorns. Brush the edge of the pastry with beaten egg.

2. Roll out the remaining pastry to a round large enough to cover the cheese. Place over the cheese, press the edges together to seal, then flute.

3. Place on a baking sheet, brush the top with beaten egg, then slash in a lattice design, taking care not to cut right through the pastry. Bake in a preheated oven, 220°C/425°F/ Gas Mark 7, for 15 minutes, until crisp and golden brown.

4. Meanwhile, make the relish. Place all the ingredients in a small pan, bring gently to the boil, then cover and simmer for about 10 minutes, until the cranberries are tender.

5. Cut the pie into 4 wedges and serve immediately, with the warm relish.

Serves 4
Preparation time: 20 minutes
Cooking time: 15 minutes
Freezing: Not recommended

SPICED PARSNIP SOUP

If the parsnips are large, discard their woody cores.

25 g (1 oz) butter
1 tablespoon oil
500 g (1 lb) parsnips,
chopped
1 onion, chopped
1 teaspoon each ground
cumin and coriander
2 teaspoons concentrated
curry paste

1 tablespoon plain flour
600 ml (1 pint) chicken
stock*
450 ml (3/4 pint) milk
142 ml (5 fl oz) carton
single cream
salt and pepper to taste
1 carrot, grated, to garnish

Serves 4
Preparation time:
15 minutes
Cooking time:
30 minutes
Freezing:
Not recommended

1. Heat the butter and oil in a large saucepan, add the parsnips and onion and stir well. Lower the heat, cover the pan and allow the vegetables to sweat for 5 minutes.
2. Stir in the cumin, coriander, curry paste and flour and cook for 1 minute, stirring well. Gradually stir in the stock and milk and bring to the boil. Season well with salt and pepper, then cover and simmer for 20 minutes, until the parsnips are tender.
3. Purée in a blender or food processor, return to the pan, add the cream and reheat gently. Divide the soup between 4 individual warmed bowls, add a little pile of grated carrot to each and sprinkle with black pepper.

POTATO AND GARLIC SOUP

Use floury potatoes for this recipe to ensure a smooth creamy texture. Despite the amount of garlic the flavour is quite subtle. Serve with croûtons* if you wish.

4 cloves garlic
750 g (1 1/2 lb) potatoes,
chopped
900 ml (1 1/2 pints) water
or chicken stock*
1 bay leaf

1/2 teaspoon saffron
strands
142 ml (5 fl oz) carton
single cream
salt and pepper to taste

Serves 4
Preparation time:
20 minutes
Cooking time:
25–30 minutes
Freezing:
Not recommended

1. Place the garlic, potatoes, water or stock, bay leaf and saffron in a large saucepan. Bring to the boil, then add salt and pepper. Cover and simmer for 25–30 minutes, until the potatoes are tender. Discard the bay leaf.
2. Purée in a blender or food processor, return to the pan and check the seasoning. Add the cream and reheat gently.

PEA AND HAM SOUP

1 bacon knuckle, weighing about 750 g (1½ lb)	*2 celery sticks, chopped*
	1 bouquet garni
250 g (8 oz) split peas, soaked overnight	*1.5 litres (2½ pints) water*
	150 ml (¼ pint) milk
1 large onion, chopped	*pepper to taste*

1. Place the bacon knuckle, peas, onion, celery, bouquet garni and water in a large pan. Bring slowly to the boil, skimming off any scum that rises to the surface, then cover and simmer for 2½ hours, until the peas are mushy and the bacon is tender.

2. Discard the bouquet garni. Remove the bacon knuckle from the pan, strip off all the meat and cut into small pieces.

3. Return the meat to the pan, add the milk and plenty of pepper and bring back to the boil. Serve piping hot.

Serves 4–6
Preparation time:
20 minutes, plus
soaking time
Cooking time:
2½ hours
Freezing:
Recommended

SPICED LENTIL SOUP

125 g (4 oz) red lentils
3 celery sticks, chopped
2 carrots, chopped
1.2 litres (2 pints) vegetable
    stock*
50 g (2 oz) bulgur wheat
    (pourgouri)
2 tablespoons oil
1 onion, chopped

1 tablespoon chopped fresh
    root ginger
1 teaspoon cumin seeds
2 teaspoons ground
    coriander
½ teaspoon turmeric
1 tablespoon lemon juice
6 tablespoons Greek yogurt
salt and pepper to taste

Serves 6
Preparation time:
20 minutes
Cooking time:
35 minutes
Freezing:
Recommended

1. Place the lentils, celery, carrots and stock in a saucepan, bring to the boil, then cover and simmer for 15 minutes. Stir in the bulgur wheat, then simmer for 15 minutes.
2. Meanwhile, heat the oil in a small pan, add the onion and fry until lightly browned. Add the ginger and cumin seeds and fry for 5 minutes. Stir in the coriander and turmeric and cook for 1 minute.
3. Stir the spices into the soup. Check the seasoning. Simmer for 5 minutes, then stir in the lemon juice. Serve hot, in bowls, with a spoonful of yogurt.

SALSIFY AND LEMON SOUP

Salsify is a long thin tapering root vegetable with a delicate flavour. Lemon not only helps it to keep its colour, but brings out its flavour too.

1.2 litres (2 pints) chicken
    or vegetable stock*
3 tablespoons lemon juice
750 g (1½ lb) salsify
2 tablespoons chopped
    celery leaves
1 onion, chopped

1 teaspoon paprika
½ bunch watercress,
    chopped finely
142 ml (5 fl oz) carton
    single cream
salt and pepper to taste

Serves 4
Preparation time:
30 minutes
Cooking time:
45–55 minutes
Freezing:
Recommended

1. Place the stock and lemon juice in a large pan. Peel the salsify and cut into 7.5 cm (3 inch) lengths, adding to the pan as you work.
2. Add the celery leaves, onion, paprika, and salt and pepper. Bring to the boil, then cover and simmer for 40–50 minutes, until the salsify is tender.
3. Purée in a blender or food processor and return to the pan. Add the watercress and cream and simmer for 5 minutes. Check the seasoning. Serve hot.

LEEK AND OATMEAL SOUP

A little oatmeal added to this winter soup makes it even more substantial and gives it a sweet, slightly nutty taste.

25 g (1 oz) butter
1 onion, chopped
2 rashers bacon, derinded
and chopped
500 g (1 lb) leeks, sliced
25 g (1 oz) fine oatmeal
900 ml (1½ pints)
vegetable stock*

300 ml (½ pint) milk
2 tablespoons chopped
parsley
75 g (3 oz) Cheddar
cheese, grated
salt and pepper to taste

Serves 4
Preparation time:
20 minutes
Cooking time:
30 minutes
Freezing:
Not recommended

1. Melt the butter in a large saucepan, add the onion and bacon and fry for about 5 minutes. Stir in the leeks and cook for 2–3 minutes. Add the oatmeal and stir well.
2. Stir in the stock, bring to the boil, then cover and simmer for 20 minutes. Purée in a blender or food processor, return to the pan, add the milk, parsley, and salt and pepper and reheat thoroughly.
3. Just before serving, stir in the cheese. Remove from the heat and continue stirring until the cheese has melted. Serve with warm wholemeal rolls.

CARROT AND CELERIAC SOUP

1 tablespoon oil
15 g (¹/₂ oz) butter or
* margarine*
2 onions, grated
350 g (12 oz) carrots,
* grated*
350 g (12 oz) celeriac,
* peeled and grated*
900 ml (1¹/₂ pints) chicken
* stock**
1 teaspoon soy sauce

1 teaspoon grated orange
* rind*
2 tablespoons freshly
* squeezed orange juice*
150 g (5.3 oz) carton set
* yogurt*
2 teaspoons cornflour,
* blended with*
* 1 tablespoon water*
chopped celery leaves to
* garnish*

1. Heat the oil and butter or margarine in a large saucepan, add the onions, carrots and celeriac and stir well. Lower the heat, cover the pan and allow the vegetables to sweat for 5 minutes.

2. Add the stock, bring to the boil, then cover and simmer for 20 minutes. Add the soy sauce, orange rind and juice and simmer for 10 minutes.

3. Mix the yogurt into the blended cornflour. Stir into the soup and simmer for 5 minutes, stirring constantly.

4. Sprinkle with celery leaves and serve with Cheese Sticks* or fingers of toast.

Serves 4
Preparation time:
20 minutes
Cooking time:
40 minutes
Freezing:
Not recommended

STOCKS & ACCOMPANIMENTS

VEGETABLE STOCK

This is a wonderful way of using up all those peelings you would normally throw away. The resulting stock is full of flavour and ideal for all vegetarian dishes, particularly risottos and main meal soups. Scrub the vegetables carefully before you peel them to remove any surface dirt.

250–350 g (8–12 oz)
* vegetable peelings, e.g.*
* potato, carrot, turnip,*
* swede*
few outer leaves from
* cabbage, lettuce, etc.*
1 large onion, chopped

1 celery stick, chopped
1 bouquet garni
6 black peppercorns
2 bay leaves
1.75 litres (3 pints) cold
* water*
salt and pepper to taste

Makes about 1.5 litres (2½ pints)
Preparation time: 10 minutes
Cooking time: 1–1½ hours
Freezing: Recommended

1. Place all the ingredients in a large saucepan and bring to the boil. Simmer, uncovered, for 1–1½ hours, until the vegetables are very tender.
2. Strain into a large bowl and leave to cool. Use as required.

CHICKEN STOCK

1 chicken carcass
1.75 litres (3 pints) cold
* water*
1 onion, quartered
few celery leaves
strip lemon rind

1 carrot, chopped
2 cloves
1 bouquet garni
6 peppercorns
salt to taste

Makes about 1.2 litres (2 pints)
Preparation time: 15 minutes
Cooking time: 2 hours
Freezing: Recommended

1. Break up the chicken carcass and place in a large saucepan with the remaining ingredients. Bring to the boil, then cover and simmer for 2 hours.
2. Strain into a bowl and leave to cool. When cold remove any surface fat with kitchen paper. Use as required.

CROÛTONS. Use white or wholemeal bread. Slice, then cut into 5 mm–1 cm (¼–½ inch) cubes or into small shapes using pastry cutters, e.g. hearts, stars. Fry in a little hot butter or oil for 4–5 minutes, until crisp and golden. Use to garnish soups.

SUFFOLK RUSKS. Use wholemeal, granary or white rolls. Pull the rolls apart and place broken side up on a baking sheet. Bake in a preheated oven, 200°C/400°F/Gas Mark 6, for 10–15 minutes, until crisp and browned. Serve warm with substantial soups or pâtés.

HOT CHEESE BREAD

1 small onion, grated
1 tablespoon chopped
parsley
75 g (3 oz) butter, softened

125 g (4 oz) Gruyère
cheese, grated finely
pepper to taste
1 long French stick

1. Mix together the onion, parsley, butter, cheese and pepper until evenly blended.
2. Cut the loaf at 2.5 cm (1 inch) intervals almost to the base. Spread the cut sides with the cheese mixture. Wrap in foil.
3. Bake in a preheated oven, 200°C/400°F/Gas Mark 6, for 15 minutes, until the cheese has melted. Serve piping hot.

Serves 4–6
Preparation time:
15 minutes
Cooking time:
15 minutes
Freezing:
Recommended, at end of stage 2

CHEESE STICKS

250 g (8 oz) ready-made
puff pastry
beaten egg for brushing

40 g (1½ oz) Parmesan
cheese, grated
salt, pepper and paprika to
taste

1. Roll out the pastry on a floured surface to 30 × 15 cm (12 × 6 inches). Brush with egg and sprinkle with one third of the cheese, and salt, pepper and paprika.
2. Fold the bottom third of the pastry up and the top third of the pastry down to cover it. Seal the edges.
3. Give the dough a quarter turn and roll out as before, sprinkling with half of the remaining cheese and the seasonings.
4. Roll out the dough to 30 × 20 cm (12 × 8 inches). Brush with egg and sprinkle with the remaining cheese and seasonings.
5. Cut the dough into 1 cm (½ inch) wide strips from one short end. Twist the strips, place on dampened baking sheets and brush with egg.
6. Bake in a preheated oven, 220°C/425°F/Gas Mark 7, for 10–12 minutes, until risen and golden. Cool on a wire rack. Serve warm.

Makes 24
Preparation time:
20 minutes
Cooking time:
10–12 minutes
Freezing:
Recommended

INDEX

Photography by: Charlie Stebbings
Designed by: Sue Storey
Home economist: Mary Cadogan
Stylist: Penny Legg
Illustration by: Linda Smith
Typeset by Rowland Phototypesetting Limited